The Heard Museum: History and Collections

**Ann E. Marshall and
Mary H. Brennan**

The Heard Museum
22 East Monte Vista Road
Phoenix, Arizona 85004

Library of Congress Catalog Number: 89-081003
ISBN: 0-934351-04-X

Maie Bartlett and Dwight Bancroft Heard, c. 1928.

The Heard Museum developed from the enthusiasm that pioneer Phoenix settlers Dwight B. and Maie Bartlett Heard felt for the Southwest, its inhabitants and its history. The Heards' dream of sharing the beauty of their collection with the public was realized in 1929 when The Heard Museum opened. Today, the Museum is internationally recognized as a place for learning about the rich cultural heritage of the American Indians of the Southwest.

"...Dwight would become one of the state's most talented leaders in journalism, finance, land development, ranching and farming. Maie would become the sponsor of social and artistic philanthropy, and together they would create a new climate in which the arts could flourish. Few couples have made such a lasting impact upon a new capital city." — C. Wesley Johnson, Jr., Director of the Phoenix History Project

Maie Bartlett was born on June 11, 1868, the oldest of four children. Her father, Adolphus Bartlett, was a major Chicago hardware wholesaler. His business, Hibbard, Spencer, and Bartlett, Co., continues today as True-Value Hardware Stores.

Dwight Heard was born May 1, 1869, in Wayland, Massachusetts, a town founded by the Heard family in 1652. Dwight's father, Leander Heard, was a partner in a wholesale grocery business. Following his father's death in 1882 and his graduation from high

school, Dwight and his widowed mother moved to Chicago. There, Dwight found employment at Hibbard, Spencer, and Bartlett, with the help of a distant relative, Adolphus Bartlett, Maie's father. The young man was welcomed into the Bartlett home and developed a friendship with Maie which, in 1893, led to their marriage.

The future in Chicago for the newlyweds was very promising. But within a year, Dwight developed a lung ailment, and doctors recommended a move to a warm and dry climate.

Throughout 1894, Dwight and Maie traveled in the West. They often carried along catalogs and hardware to sell for Hibbard, Spencer, and Bartlett. Their search for a new home ended when they visited Phoenix, Arizona. The desert community impressed them so much that they decided to put down permanent roots.

b.

a.

a. The evening wedding of Maie Bartlett and Dwight Heard was held on August 10, 1893, in Chicago, at the Prairie Avenue home of the bride's father. The *Chicago Tribune* referred to the occasion as "the only large wedding of the midsummer season."

b. When the Heards arrived in Phoenix from Chicago in 1895, there were approximately 4,000 residents. The town had become the capitol of the Arizona Territory only six years earlier. This photo, c. 1900, looks north up Center Street (now Central Avenue) at Adams Street. To the right is the Adams Hotel, built by John C. Adams, another Chicagoan. Dwight Heard's first office building was located on Center across from the hotel.

3

"Phoenix's most familiar image of Mrs. Heard was of a diminutive, spirited social worker, listing under the weight of a briefcase crammed with minutes and reports of her organizations, as she scurried from meeting to meeting." — Orme Lewis, Phoenix attorney and former President, The Heard Museum Board of Trustees.

Once settled in Phoenix, Mrs. Heard began a profound and lifelong interest in the cultural betterment of the Salt River Valley. She was actively involved with the founding or support of a number of civic endeavors, including the Boy Scouts, Camp Fire Girls, the YWCA, and the Woman's Club of Phoenix. Mrs. Heard and other Bartlett family members donated land for the city's first civic center at the corner of Central Avenue and McDowell Road.

a.

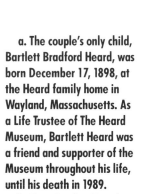

b.

"Arizona's foremost citizen... a man who devoted his energy and ability to the upbuilding of his adopted city and state." — *Arizona Republican,* March 16, 1929

Mr. Heard wanted his new hometown to flourish. Through his business connections and those of his father-in-law, he encouraged eastern investors to look at Phoenix and the Salt River Valley. His investment company, which specialized in real estate, became an important factor in the economic development of the area.

Mr. Heard was one of the largest landowners in the Salt River Valley. His interests included the Bartlett-Heard Land and Cattle Company south of Phoenix where he raised prize cattle, alfalfa, citrus trees, and cotton. As the president of the Arizona Cotton Growers' Association, he is credited with helping to make the Arizona cotton growers industry competitive internationally.

As one who was interested in the development of the Salt River Valley, Dwight Heard was a central figure in the issue of water reclamation in the West. He recognized water as a key to growth in the region and was instrumental in bringing water to the Arizona desert. Travels to Egypt convinced him that development of an irrigation system was essential to agriculture, and he helped to establish the Salt River Water Users' Association.

Mr. Heard entered the newspaper business with the purchase of the *Arizona Republican* in October 1912. As publisher, he saw the newspaper's role as one of promoting internal interests of Arizona for the betterment of the state.

b.

a.

a. Dwight Heard planted palm trees on his estate and on his other properties. This c. 1910 photo shows Mr. Heard standing next to a Sago palm.

b. Dwight Heard confers with Democratic Governor George W. P. Hunt at an Illinois reunion picnic in 1913. Hunt had been elected the previous year as the first governor of the state of Arizona. In 1924, Mr. Heard ran unsuccessfully for governor against Hunt.

"Nothing was ever done in that house informally." — Winifred Heard, daughter-in-law of the Heards

In 1903, the Heards built an elegant home in North Central Phoenix, which they named "Casa Blanca." Visitors entered a sweeping circular driveway that began with a decorative fence with "Casa Blanca" in raised letters. The one-story, 6,000-square-foot house had six fireplaces and was built around an open courtyard. The entire estate included a gazebo, clay tennis court, a palm tree nursery, and later, an adjacent two-story guest house.

In order to create the finest housing development in Phoenix, Mr. Heard bought 160 acres of property along Central Avenue north of McDowell Road. Here he developed Los Olivos, an exclusive residential area. The couple beautified the development by planting hundreds of palm trees along four miles of roads in Los Olivos, and are credited with introducing the stately trees to Phoenix.

The Heards were known for entertaining. They staged Shakespearean readings on the front lawn of Casa Blanca, and held costume parties. Guests at Casa Blanca included notable state and national figures. The Heards were hosts to two U.S. presidents, Herbert Hoover and Theodore Roosevelt, and prominent business people, including Chicago retailer Marshall Field. Her husband's many contacts and spontaneous invitations required Mrs. Heard to put together dinners and parties at a moment's notice. To ensure the household ran smoothly, Mrs. Heard supervised a staff of one cook, two maids, and two gardeners.

Inside Casa Blanca, maple-floored rooms were filled with furnishings and accessories gathered on the couple's travels.

b.

The Heards' home, Casa Blanca, was a Phoenix showplace, centrally located in Dwight Heard's prestigious Los Olivos development. The Heards beautified the estate with palm trees and colorful flowers. (opposite page)

a. A brochure, c.1911, advertises Dwight Heard's Los Olivos development. The album belonged to Fred Bancroft, a cousin of Dwight Heard who had visited at Casa Blanca and taken many family snapshots.

b. President Theodore Roosevelt waves from a car in front of Casa Blanca with Maie Bartlett Heard in the background. He visited Arizona on several occasions, including the 1911 dedication of Roosevelt Dam and a 1916 stay as a house guest at Casa Blanca.

a.

a.

"They were interested in Indian art from the beginning. They had a mutual interest in culture and the background of Arizona native peoples."
— Bartlett Heard, the Heards' son

The Heards began collecting American Indian artifacts soon after their move to Phoenix in 1895. They were a team in this mutual interest, although Mrs. Heard was most immediately involved with shaping the collection. The Heards extended their collecting to other cultures outside North America, including Egypt

a. Baskets, pots, and textiles, much of it executed by American Indians, were used extensively for decorating the interior of Casa Blanca, as seen in this photo, c. 1910.

b. Now a part of the permanent collection of The Heard Museum, this Western Apache basket was once displayed on the fireplace mantle in the Heards' home.

b.

and Hawaii, building their collection through travel and contacts with trading posts, and Indian arts dealers, including the Fred Harvey Company.

In light of their interest in American Indian culture, in December 1926, the Heards purchased a piece of property in Phoenix at 19th Street and Polk Street that was the site of Hohokam Indian ruins. They hired Frank Midvale, an amateur archaeologist, to excavate the ruins called "La Ciudad." The site was shared with the public through a series of afternoon viewings for several years.

Mr. Heard was particularly interested in prehistory, especially La Ciudad. He was a speaker on the subject at Rotary Clubs throughout the Phoenix area. He also arranged for the exhibiting of examples of prehistoric southwestern pottery in the windows of the Heard Investment Company in downtown Phoenix.

b.

a.

a. The Heard family and friends enjoy a spring outing to prehistoric cliff dwellings, c. 1910. Maie Bartlett Heard is on the far right and Bartlett Heard is second from the left.

b. Dwight Heard is pictured with a worker at the excavation of La Ciudad, a Hohokam archaeological site in Phoenix that was owned by the Heards.

Ultimately, the size of the collection began to suggest to the Heards that it could and should become a community resource. It has been reported that daughter-in-law Winifred Heard first gave the Heards the idea of opening a formal museum for their collection.

A completely separate structure for the Museum was required on the grounds of the Casa Blanca estate. The couple worked closely with noted architect Herbert Green to create a Spanish Colonial Revival design that complemented both the adjacent Casa Blanca and the southwestern climate.

The Heards' collection was installed in twelve exhibit galleries on two floors clustered around a court-yard that looks much the same today. Visitors to The Heard Museum could see American Indian material from the western United States, and as far north as Point Barrow, Alaska. Far away places that the Heards had visited, including Hawaii and Africa, were also represented in exhibits.

Although the Heards had begun the Museum together, only Mrs. Heard would live to see it open. Mr. Heard died on March 14, 1929, following a heart attack, several months before the opening of the Museum.

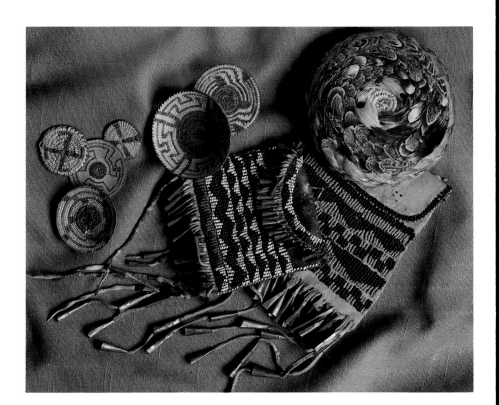

Miniature Pima baskets and Western Apache bead-work from Arizona, and feathered Pomo baskets from California were described by 1929 news-paper accounts as the type of materials exhibited at The Heard Museum.

a.

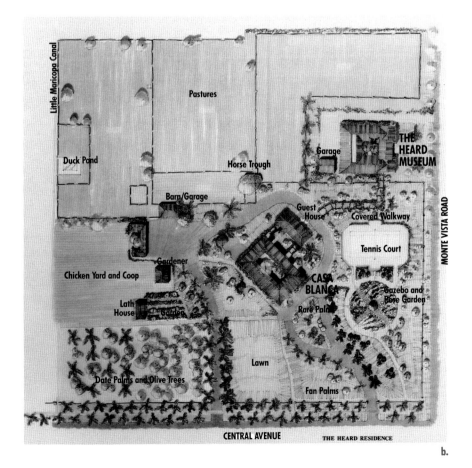

Little Maricopa Canal

Pastures

Duck Pond

Horse Trough

Garage

THE HEARD MUSEUM

Barn/Garage

Guest House

Covered Walkway

Tennis Court

MONTE VISTA ROAD

Chicken Yard and Coop

Gardener

CASA BLANCA

Lath House

Garden

Rare Palms

Gazebo and Rose Garden

Date Palms and Olive Trees

Lawn

Fan Palms

CENTRAL AVENUE   THE HEARD RESIDENCE

b.

a. The Heard Museum is pictured shortly after completion. The absence of any sign indicating the building's name suggests a quiet beginning for the institution.

b. This map of Casa Blanca, the Heards' suburban estate, indicates the location of the Museum building in relation to the main house. The two structures were linked by a covered walkway.

Instead of retiring to a quiet life when her husband died, Maie Heard chose to go on with the Museum project and filed the Articles of Incorporation on June 18, 1929.

Mrs. Heard played an active role in the Museum. Frequently, in the early days, visitors to the Museum would first ring the door bell at Casa Blanca. Mrs. Heard would answer and take the visitors over to the Museum, unlock the gate, and give them a tour. She also made it a regular habit to take artifacts, such as baskets and pottery, home to Casa Blanca so she could give them a thorough cleaning.

From the beginning, under the guidance of Mrs. Heard, The Heard Museum was interested in general public education. Regularly scheduled lectures were held to explain the exhibits to visitors, Saturday storytelling sessions were held for children, speakers from the Museum visited the schools, and schools were invited to have their students tour the Museum and its exhibits.

Mrs. Heard died on March 14, 1951, but the legacy begun by both she and her husband, continues to the present with The Heard Museum and its sharing of American Indian cultures and art.

Mrs. Heard joins Eagle Scout Tom Fannin in admiring a prehistoric jar found by the scouts while camping on private property. The c. 1943 newspaper photo was published with the caption "Adventure of a Lifetime."

a.

b.

a. The Museum's central courtyard was the site of a concert in the early years.

b. Articles from April and November 1940 issues of the *Arizona Republic,* record appreciative audiences for lectures by a young Barry Goldwater at The Heard Museum. The lectures were presented in the Museum's first auditorium, now the Sandra Day O'Connor Lounge.

Since its founding, The Heard Museum has presented the art and artifacts of people from many different parts of the world. American Indian cultures have always been a primary interest, particulary those from the southwestern United States.

As a Museum, collecting and preserving art and artifacts of the past and present are important activities. They are a starting point for learning about the people who used the artifacts and created the art.

The Museum's public programs, exhibits, and annual events focus on providing opportunities for people from many cultures to meet and talk.

American Indian artists are frequently available in the Museum galleries to answer questions about their art and culture. The DeGrazia Foundation of Tucson has sponsored many of these artists. Performing artists presenting dance, music, and poetry from many cultures are also part of Museum programs.

From the Museum's opening in 1929 until her death in 1951, Mrs. Heard worked to establish the solid foundation on which today's Museum

Annually, volunteer guides at The Heard Museum provide tours for more than 16,000 school children and 36,000 adults.

has been built. Since 1951, a series of volunteer Boards of Trustees have guided and supported the Museum's growth from a family institution to a major cultural organization. Much of the Museum's growth has been made possible by volunteers.

The formation of volunteer support groups has created expanded educational opportunities for Museum visitors and the community. One of these groups is The Heard Museum Guild. Since its founding in 1956, The Guild has increased from 30 members to 700, and now provides a substantial portion of Museum support through major donations of talent, hours, and money. The efforts of the Guild are directed toward the development of the Museum, and its members assist in education programs, library services, and curatorial and collections procedures. The Guild's Speakers Bureau brings the Museum to the community, and the Guild's Las Guias program provides guides for public and private tours. The Guild also staffs the Information Desk and the Museum Shop and Bookstore.

b.

a.

a. Performances by American Indian groups of the Southwest, such as this Western Apache *Gaan* dancer, are a high point of the annual Heard Museum Guild Indian Fair. Every March during the Guild Indian Fair, thousands of visitors from all over the world have their first opportunity to watch traditional dances, talk with craftspersons, and taste American Indian foods.

b. Wendy Weston Ben (Navajo), a DeGrazia Artist in Residence at the Museum, is shown demonstrating the art of beadworking in one of the galleries.

"Family Blackboard" by Jane Ash Poitras (Cree), of Edmonton, Alberta, Canada, was exhibited in The Heard Museum 4th Biennial Native American Fine Arts Invitational. The general theme of the collage is the artist's personal statement on the "education of Indians."

The Guild also sponsors a number of annual events, including a fair, lecture series, and a juried exhibit and sale of art by American Indian student artists.

The Heard Men's Council is another of the Museum's volunteer support groups. The Men's Council assists the Board of Trustees and Museum staff in furthering the educational programs of the Museum and performing fund raising activities. It has sponsored the prestigious Biennial Native American Fine Arts Invitational, which showcases upcoming American Indian artists and attracts fine art collectors from all over the country. The Men's Council is also active in membership development.

Through its volunteer support groups, the Museum presents a wide range of public programs and special events. These programs exist through the generosity of many people in the community of friends who give freely of their time and talent. These volunteer groups are always interested in hearing from people who want to join in the many projects of the Museum.

"We have lived upon this land from days beyond history's record, far past any living memory, deep into the time of legend. The story of my people and the story of this place are one single story. No man can think of us without thinking of this place." — A Taos Pueblo man.

Native Peoples of the Southwest is a journey through time and across the landscape of the American Southwest. This major exhibit, which is the most extensive of its kind in North America, presents the history of southwestern Native America—the land, and the people and their cultural and artistic achievements. Many traditions and cultures have flourished in the desert, uplands, and plateau areas. The Museum's collection of artifacts made by these people are presented in this exhibit.

The Heard Museum draws on its own extensive collection or loaned collections to present an active schedule of changing exhibits. Several major galleries are dedicated to presenting special exhibits.

a.

b.

a. This topographical relief map in *Native Peoples of the Southwest* highlights the three exhibit areas — the Sonoran Desert, the Uplands Region of the Southwest, and the Colorado Plateau.

b. Panoramic vistas of the Southwest landscape, mingled with powerful images of American Indian people and their culture, are part of a unique audio-visual program, "Our Voices, Our Land." The voices of American Indians tell the story of the deep relationship between the land and its people, pay tribute to their ancestors, and express hopes for the future.

American Indian fine art is always displayed at the Museum. Special exhibits of painting, drawing, prints, photography, and sculpture are presented in the Gallery of Indian Art. The exhibits reflect the scope of the Museum collection which contains historic drawings more than a century old, as well as contemporary canvases. In addition, visitors may see special traveling exhibits that the Museum has arranged to present.

Interactive exhibits that include "hands-on" activities are an important feature of the Museum. "Hands-on" activities extend learning beyond traditional museum viewing. The activities may include working with natural fibers, composing a blanket design, or playing a musical instrument. The interactive exhibits are enjoyable for children and are good family activities.

b.

a. Young visitors to The Heard Museum enjoy the sound of a drum in a hands-on exhibit that affords first-hand experiences with American Indian culture.

b. The Gallery of American Indian Art showcases traditional and contemporary fine art by American Indian artists.

Museum exhibits sometimes include American Indian house types, such as this *tipi* that visitors can step inside. (opposite page)

a.

a.

Several of the loveliest areas of the Museum are located outdoors. Immediately adjacent to the galleries is The Dr. Dean Nichols Sculpture Court. The desert setting is an ideal place for visitors to enjoy works of art and appreciate some excellent examples of desert plants. The sculptures in this area include works from the Museum's collection, as well as works available for sale.

North of the Museum building, the J. Lester Shaffer Green offers a perfect setting for contemporary sculp-

a. A variety of performing arts events are held in the Scott L. Libby, Jr. Amphitheater.

b. The Dr. Dean Nichols Sculpture Court, with its filtered shade, is a pleasant place for visitors to rest.

b.

tures by such widely recognized American Indian artists as Allan Houser, Bob Haozous, and Doug Hyde.

The Scott L. Libby, Jr. Amphitheater, adjacent to the Shaffer Green, is equipped with state-of-the-art sound and lighting systems that allow for a variety of day and evening performances. This amphitheater permits the Museum to move beyond the presentation of visual arts. The performing arts —dance, song, instrumental music, and oratory—are an integral part of Museum programs, for which the amphitheater provides an excellent setting.

The Heard Museum Shop and Bookstore displays southwestern American Indian crafts, fine art, and literary works. The gallery-style store offers traditional items such as pottery, jewelry, baskets, textiles, and kachina dolls, as well as more contemporary works of fine art. The Bookstore contains a wide selection of books by and about the American Indian and books on art and historical and geographical materials. The Bookstore serves as a valuable resource for educators and researchers, as well as for visitors to the Museum.

The Museum's first shop was begun in 1958 as a fund raising project of the Heard Museum Guild. Since opening, the shop has always been staffed by volunteers from the Guild. Guild volunteers participate in special training workshop and continuing education programs to ensure they can serve customers with a maximum amount of information about the available art and the American Indian artists.

b.

a. The Heard Museum Shop and Bookstore offers southwestern arts and crafts by contemporary American Indian artists.

b. "Chiricahua Apache Family," 1983, is by noted American Indian sculptor Allan Houser. The sculpture, located on the J. Lester Shaffer Green, is on loan from the Glenn Green Galleries.

a.

By the mid 1920s, Mr. and Mrs. Heard were transforming a personal collection into a museum collection. The earliest records retained with the collection are receipts for purchases at Indian arts stores. Dealers throughout the Southwest wrote to the Heards offering special pieces for sale. Most frequently, the material purchased was an example of American Indian craft art. The Heards seemed to be shaping an educational collection that showed some of the variety present within these craft arts in addition to acquiring items of quality.

From 1924 to 1929, Herbert BraMé and his wife Alice were employed by the Heards to acquire artifacts for the collection. BraMé, owner of the Arizona Curio Company in Prescott, was a wholesaler of Indian arts. Mrs. Heard maintained an account with BraMé, who purchased things for her approval and received a ten percent commission on sales.

In the five years he worked for the Heards, BraMé primarily collected material from the West. Occasional purchases went farther afield, including Yaqui artifacts from Northwest Mexico and even a few Pacific artifacts.

An early catalog of the Museum collection, which was probably maintained through Mrs. Heard's lifetime, lists more than 3,000 cataloged pieces.

b.

a. The Heards purchase baskets in the Sudan on their 1925 trip on the Nile River.

b. Receipts from the Arizona Curio Company and other dealers show purchases of American Indian material in the 1920s by the Heards.

a.

Prehistoric Hohokam artifacts from excavations at the Heards' archaeological site, La Ciudad, were most numerous. Basketry was the second largest category of items with almost 800 baskets recorded in the collection.

Historic and contemporary ceramics from the Rio Grande Pueblos of New Mexico, and from other Arizona and New Mexico cultures, were important to the collection. Seventy-four utilitarian and decorative ceramics from Hopi composed slightly over one-half of the early collection. The Museum owned works by Maria Martinez and her sister, Anna, of San Ildefonso, and Maricopa potter Mary Juan, as well as work attributed to Nampeyo. In making such purchases, Mrs. Heard was collecting superior works from potters who were contemporary with her time.

Mrs. Heard collected many examples of American Indian beadwork from the West. When the Museum opened in 1929, a major portion of one gallery exhibited Western Apache beadwork. Mrs. Heard's sister, Florence Dibell Bartlett, was also a contributor of beaded items in the early years of the Museum.

Navajo textiles were prominent in the early Museum collection. Approximately 100 Navajo textiles in the Museum collection were probably acquired under Mrs. Heard's supervision. They include a few wearing blankets and serapes from the 1860s and 1870s, excellent Germantown textiles from the 1880s, and some pieces that were contemporary when collected.

Mrs. Heard collected jewelry only in a limited way. The original collection contained about 60 pieces, of which 49 were Navajo.

These artifacts — a Chilkat blanket, a Western Apache basket, and a Santa Clara blackware wedding jar — are part of the Museum's early collection. The blanket is from Alaska and was obtained from the Hudson Bay Company in the 1920s. The basket was in the Heards' personal collection by 1910. Museum records do not indicate the date on which the wedding vase was purchased, but its original price was $15.

23

Jewelry

American Indian jewelry from the Southwest is primarily recognized for distinctive styling of silver, turquoise, and other colorful stones and shell. The use of turquoise and shell in jewelry dates to prehistoric times. Techniques for working silver were learned primarily from Mexican silversmiths during the 1850s through the 1880s.

The jewelry traditions of three cultures: Navajo, Zuni, and Hopi, are in the Museum collection and exhibits. The collection also contains examples of turquoise and shell jewelry from the Rio Grande Pueblos of New Mexico.

Turquoise is a distinctive feature of southwestern jewelry. The importance of turquoise for the Navajo exceeds its use in jewelry and extends to the most profound Navajo religious beliefs. Turquoise in jewelry is used in different styles by Navajo and Zuni jewelers. Navajo smiths have traditionally used large stones set in beautifully wrought silver settings. Zuni jewelers have worked with designs that cluster many shaped

stones together. Modern jewelers continue to feature turquoise while exploring a variety of other materials, including gold, and precious and semi-precious stones.

Navajo silver jewelry, of which the Museum collection contains more than 1,000 pieces, represents a mastery of silverworking combined with dramatic selection from the many varieties of turquoise. Forms taken by Navajo silverwork have changed through the years. Some silverwork from the late 1800s and early 1900s, such as horse trappings, blouse ornaments, bowguards, and tobacco canteens, are less

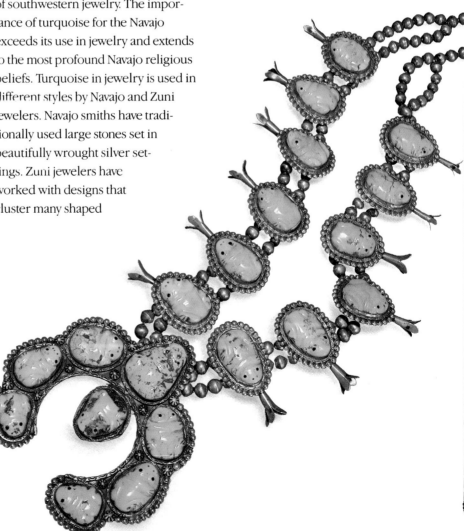

This squash blossom necklace with turquoise frogs displays the talent of a noted Zuni carver, Leakay Deysee. Made in 1939, it is from the collection of C. G. Wallace, now a part of the permanent holdings of The Heard Museum.

frequently produced today. But many more forms from the early 20th century have a classic style and appeal. The distinctive squash blossom necklace, band bracelet, and concha belt are widely appreciated today.

Silver jewelry was made at Hopi in the early 1900s, but distinctively styled jewelry using the overlay technique began in the 1930s. Overlay refers to the cutting of designs into a silver sheet that is placed on top of a solid silver backing. The cut-out area is oxidized to blacken and accent the design.

If superbly styled silver work distinguishes Navajo and Hopi jewelry, Zuni jewelry's most striking feature is intricate lapidary work. Turquoise, jet, coral, and shell form complex mosaic patterns, delicate needlepoint designs, and distinctive animal fetish necklaces. The contrasting colors of stone and shell are often used in a pictorial or representational style by Zuni jewelers. The Museum collection includes more than 400 examples of work by noted Zuni jewelers.

b.

c.

a.

a. This buckle was made by Paul Saufkie and is believed to be an early example of Hopi overlay done shortly after World War II.

b. Concha belts are a classic type of southwestern jewelry. These belts were made by Navajo silversmiths. The middle belt was made by Roger Skeet who used turquoise bears carved by Zuni artist Leakay Deysee.

c. These turquoise and shell necklaces in the Museum's collection were probably produced by Pueblo jewelers, but worn and appreciated by the Navajo.

25

Textiles

a.

American Indian weaving traditions in the Southwest are the Navajo and Pueblo. Of the two, the Pueblo is the older with a heritage from prehistoric times. The Museum's collection contains approximately 1,300 textiles, of which more than 700 are examples of Navajo weaving.

Navajo weaving is best known and most prized from the 19th century. Navajo textiles from this period had a variety of uses including clothing and bedding. Among the most highly regarded weavings were shoulder blankets and serapes in bold designs. Some of these blankets were prized as trade items far beyond the Southwest.

By the late 1800s, commercial blankets and cloth replaced many traditional uses for weaving. Reservation traders encouraged Navajo women to weave rugs that could be sold in the

a. The Museum continues to collect contemporary examples of Pueblo weaving and embroidery. This Hopi sash was made in 1974.

b. The exhibit, *Native Peoples of the Southwest,* presents some of the oldest Navajo textiles in the Museum's collection. All but the Germantown textile (far left), which is a floor covering, were woven as shoulder blankets or ponchos.

b.

East and to the growing tourist trade. Using commercial yarn in bright colors, some weavers produced intricately patterned textiles known as "eyedazzlers."

During the early part of the 20th century, most Navajo weaving took the form of rugs in natural wool colors with accents of red yarn of handspun wool dyed with packaged chemical dyes. Many of these rugs were sold by traders and wholesalers through catalog promotion. Designs were in many cases originally derived from the oriental rug designs that were more familiar to potential customers.

By the mid 1900s, Navajo weavers were executing regionally distinct styles that drew on older designs. Some were a revival of horizontal banded designs with pastel vegetal dyed yarns. Others elaborated the bordered oriental rug designs or combined them with Hispanic serape motifs. These distinctive designs were historically associated with an area of the reservation or a trading post. Names of some regional styles include: Two Grey Hills, Ganado, Crystal, Chinle, Teec Nos Pos, Wide Ruins, and Burnt Water.

Navajo weavers continue to develop new design styles that display novel color combinations. The innovation that has always characterized Navajo weaving remains a primary feature today.

By contrast, from the 1800s to the present, textiles produced in Pueblo cultures have changed very little with regard to design. Unlike Navajo weaving, these textiles have not been produced in any quantity for sale with the exception of woven belts. Many Pueblo textiles are associated with ceremony. Embroidered kilts, robes, and sashes are worn by dancers in ceremonies as are knitted leggings.

This child-size serape or wearing blanket is an example of Navajo design, c. 1870.

Ceramics

The Heard Museum's ceramic collection focuses on more than 3,500 examples of southwestern ceramics from prehistory to the present. Prehistoric Pueblo people produced ceramics of striking diversity and beauty. This heritage of ceramic artistry has continued through time to present-day people living at Hopi, Zuni, Acoma, and the Rio Grande Pueblos of New Mexico.

Historic Pueblo ceramics include many pieces used for food storage, preparation, and serving. Made by a coil-and-scrape process, the ceramics were painted with animal, floral, and geometric designs. The designs were often distinctive of the Pueblo in which the piece was made. Production of some of these utilitarian wares decreased as manufactured metal containers became more common in the late 19th century. But, ceramics continued to be manufactured for sale to increasing numbers of tourists visiting the Southwest.

Changes within the 20th century include production of smaller pieces, design innovation, increasingly perfected surface polish, revival of prehistoric designs, and surface treatments. One of the most popular surface treatments is on polished blackware produced at the New Mexico Pueblos of San Ildefonso and Santa Clara.

In recent years, some ceramicists have looked to miniaturization as a challenging area of work. Some of these miniatures are decorated with detailed figures carved into the surface in a process called sgraffito. A few Hopi artists have developed uniquely colored and shaped pieces. In the Southwest, the ceramic tradition continues to change as artists explore their medium.

a. These Mimbres bowls, c.1000-1150, are decorated with designs that tell a story.

b. This small ceramic jar with a bold design was probably made by the Hopi-Tewa potter, Nampeyo, c. 1920. In the 1890s, Nampeyo revived designs based on ancient pottery styles. Ceramics from this period were primarily made to be sold to collectors.

c. This ceramic "Storyteller" figure by Helen Cordero of Cochiti Pueblo in New Mexico was made in 1969.

These contemporary blackware jars are by artists from the New Mexico Pueblos of Santa Clara and San Ildefonso: (clockwise from right) Rose Gonzales, Joseph Lonewolf, Teresita Naranjo, and Margaret Tafoya. The bear paw is distinctive of Santa Clara ceramics, while the serpent is commonly seen on ceramics from Santa Clara and San Ildefonso. (opposite page)

b.

c.

Quillwork and Beadwork

Porcupine quills and bird feather quills have been used to ornament clothing, pouches and other containers, and home furnishings of many American Indian cultures in the eastern United States and the Great Plains. Some cultures on the Plains who lived where there were no porcupines traded to obtain quills.

The introduction of glass beads from Europe by traders and explorers partially supplanted quill decoration. Colorful glass beads could be used to achieve designs similar to those of dyed quills. But, quills continued to be used as ornament in conjunction with beads and remain today a distinctively American Indian craft art.

In Arizona, Western Apache clothing was ornamented with beads that were also used for necklaces. Yuman tribes of the Lower Colorado River made shawl collars of beads. But, articles with beadwork and quillwork were not made as extensively in the Southwest as in the Great Plains, the Plateau region of Montana and Idaho, and the eastern United States.

Some beaded and quilled artifacts are associated with babies and small children. Cradleboard covers of many cultures from the Great Plains are almost entirely covered with beads or colorfully dyed quills.

Quillwork and beadwork are also the principal means of ornamenting the dramatic regalia worn in contemporary Pow-wow activities. Beadwork and quillwork today are vibrant craft arts that express the valued heritage of many American Indians.

The Heard Museum collection contains more than 600 examples of beadwork and quillwork, primarily from cultures of the Great Plains.

Fully beaded cradleboards were made by several tribes of the Great Plains. This cradleboard is Kiowa from the Southern Plains, c. 1890.

a.

b.

a. These Great Plains pipe bags were made by the Cheyenne, Sioux, and Kiowa, c. 1890-1920.

b. A Kiowa girl's dress of buckskin is ornamented with glass seed beads, elk teeth, cowrie shells, and ribbon, c.1890. In addition, it is painted with green pigment made from algae and yellow made from bison gallstones.

Baskets

a. The Fred Harvey Company collected baskets from the Pacific Northwest. This c. 1900 Tlingit basket from Alaska is unusual because it is a pictorial design, specifically of a killer whale.

b. The Heards lived nearest to Pima basket weavers. Mrs. Heard had a collection of approximately 200 miniature Pima baskets.

Baskets are among the earliest containers in the West, predating pottery. Baskets were often the basic containers for food gathering and preparation. Some baskets were even made to hold liquids. In Arizona, groups like the Western Apache coated baskets with pitch and used them as water bottles. By the early 1900s, many of these utilitarian baskets were no longer being made because manufactured containers were available.

Some basketmakers continued to weave baskets for sale. During the early 1900s, basket collecting was a popular hobby. Many visitors to the West wanted a basket as a souvenir of their trip. Basketmakers adapted their technical knowledge to the new uses for baskets.

Many baskets were made smaller with flat bases, and were useful as letter baskets or sewing baskets. Large, jar-shaped baskets were used as waste baskets or umbrella stands. Miniature baskets were popular, as were baskets with designs featuring distinctive animals or plants of the region.

The same skill and knowledge of nature was required to produce the baskets made for sale. As with other American Indian craft arts whose raw materials are gathered in nature, much knowledge and time is necessary to begin work on a piece. Materials for American Indian baskets are harvested from growing plants. A basketmaker needs to know where the useful plants are located, how and when to harvest the fibers, and how to prepare the fibers.

Baskets in the collection of The Heard Museum include approximately 2,500 from southwestern American Indian cultures. Baskets from many cultures of California, the Great Basin, and the Northwest are also well represented in the Museum collection.

a.

b.

a.

b.

a. Western Apache bas-
ketmakers created large
baskets in the shapes of jars
or urns. This piece was collected at San Carlos Reservation in southeastern Arizona
between 1890-1930.

b. *Native Peoples of the
Southwest* presents many
baskets from the Museum's
collection including baskets
from the Uplands cultures of
the Havasupai and Hualapai
(on the left) and the Western
Apache (on the right). A traditional Western Apache
shelter is also shown.

The Heard Museum's collection of kachina dolls includes more than 1,200 examples from the past 100 years. Kachina dolls are carvings of religious figures traditionally produced at the Pueblos of Hopi, Zuni, and some Rio Grande Pueblos. At Hopi, kachina dolls are gifts to little girls. They are given with a prayer-wish for future growth and well-being. Girls usually receive dolls during ceremonies held in February and July. In addition to this traditional purpose, kachina dolls have increasingly been carved for sale.

Hopi dolls are made of cottonwood root. Over the years the general style of carving and painting has changed. Dolls from the turn of the century often have a solid body with legs and arms defined, but not separate. The old dolls may have a neck ruff of Douglas fir, carefully embroidered or appliqued clothing, and are painted with mineral pigments. Dolls from the mid 1900s are carved in poses that suggest movement. They are colorful with various types of poster paint or oil-based paint used to indicate clothing. Some are carefully feathered and ornamented.

The most recent dolls continue to be examples of action sculpture. They may be entirely carved of wood with all details of feathers, hair, cloth, and plants detailed in wood. The color of these newest dolls is often a stain that permits the wood grain to show through.

Kachina dolls carved at Zuni are stylistically distinct from Hopi dolls. Zuni carvings traditionally have elongated bodies and faces, more clothing made of cloth, and wooden arms made of separate pieces attached to the body. Zuni dolls have not been carved and sold as a craft art to the same extent as at Hopi.

a. More than 500 Hopi kachina dolls collected by the Fred Harvey Company and Senator Barry M. Goldwater are on exhibit in a special gallery within *Native Peoples of the Southwest.*

b. This Zuni kachina doll, c. 1920s, is a *Sha'lako* doll. The *Sha'lako* have been described as "Giant Courier Gods of the Rainmakers."

These Hopi kachina dolls represent figures in the "Going Home" ceremony that takes place after the summer solstice. The dolls in the rear wear distinctive wooden headdresses called *tabletas.* (opposite page)

© 1984, Al Payne

a.

b.

Special Collections of American Indian Ethnographic Arts

This Hopi kachina doll by White Bear Fredericks is called *Sakwahote.* The Kachina this doll represents appears in dances of the spring and summer that are held in the village plazas.

The Heard Museum has been the fortunate recipient of several major collections that focus on western, especially southwestern American Indian material. Frequently known by the collector's name, these holdings have greatly extended the range of ideas the Museum can present through its exhibits. These collections are listed in order of acquisition.

The Goldwater Kachina Doll Collection, developed by Senator Barry M. Goldwater, was donated to The Heard Museum in 1964. The Museum collection of Hopi kachina dolls was a modest one until Senator Goldwater donated his 437 doll collection. The dolls range in date of manufacture from the late 1800s to the early 1960s. Some of Senator Goldwater's older dolls were originally acquired by John Kibbey, a Phoenix architect who introduced seven-year-old Goldwater to the Hopi culture in 1916. Following World War II, Senator Goldwater acquired Kibbey's collection and added it to his own. In an effort to collect examples of the many different Hopi kachina dolls, Senator Goldwater commissioned the Hopi carver, Oswald White Bear Fredericks, to make approximately 90 dolls for his collection.

In 1971, a collection developed by Byron Harvey III, great grandson of the founder of the Fred Harvey Company, was donated to the Museum. The collection includes more than 1,200 ethnographic and archaeological artifacts primarily from Southwest and Plains Indian cultures. Mr. Harvey's knowledge of anthropology and the Southwest guided him in shaping a very important collection. Mr. Harvey has continued to donate to the collection, particularly cradleboards and historic photographs in recent years. The Harvey family, through the subsequent donation of the Fred Harvey Company Fine Arts Collection, has played a major role in expanding the Museum collections.

Travelers on the Santa Fe Railroad discovered the West and American Indian cultures through the Fred Harvey Company. Founded in 1876 to provide food and lodging along the rail line, the company established its Indian Department in 1902. The principal buyer, Herman Schweizer, acquired American Indian craft arts to be sold in the Company's gift shops. Schweizer also acquired pieces of extraordinary quality for the Company's special collection. In 1978, the Harvey family donated this American Indian collection and some Hispanic artifacts to The Heard Museum. The collection contains more than 4,000 examples of western American Indian ceramics, textiles, basketry, beadwork, jewelry, and ethnographic material. It represents a major addition to The Heard Museum collection, not only in terms of its considerable quality but also for extending the collection's strength in major southwestern American Indian craft arts back into the last half of the 19th century.

a.

b.

c.

a. Contemporary Navajo textiles from the collection of Read Mullan include a Ganado by Alice Begay, a Teec Nos Pos by Dee Etsitty, and a Wide Ruins rug by Lottie Thompson.

b. Hopi jewelry from the Galbraith Collection includes works by noted silversmiths. The quail pin by Ralph Tawangyaouma is an early piece, c. 1930, while the buckle by Victor Coochwy-tewa and the bracelet by Lawrence Saufkie are more recent.

c. An Assiniboin cradle cover, donated by Byron Harvey, III, is almost entirely covered with tiny glass beads, called seed beads, that were imported from Europe.

Donated in 1975, the C.G. Wallace Collection has more than 500 pieces of jewelry, primarily Zuni, augmented by 138 Navajo pieces. The jewelry dates from the 1920s through the 1940s, and is extremely important because many of the pieces are identified as to maker and date of production. Mr. Wallace, a trader in the Zuni and Gallup areas for more than 50 years, was an integral part of the development of Zuni jewelry production and marketing. His collection includes works by the best jewelers of Zuni from that time period.

The Read Mullan Collection of Navajo Textiles consists of nearly 90 rugs donated to The Heard Museum in 1976. Mr. Mullan was a prominent Phoenix car dealer and Trustee of The Heard Museum. These textiles are nearly all contemporary weavings produced between 1950 and 1970. A few exceptions include four rare sandpainting rugs dating to the 1920s and 1930s. The textiles are excellent in quality, most having won prizes at major competitions in Arizona and New Mexico.

In 1979, the Friends of Mexican Art, (FOMA), made funds available to purchase more than 355 artifacts from Northwest Mexico. The collection assembled by Edmund Faubert was intended to expand the Museum's focus on the Southwest by improving its collection of artifacts from cultures that are from the neighboring northwestern region of Mexico.

In 1980, the Museum received the Plummer Collection from a California family. The total collection encompasses more than 800 ethnographic items, but nearly 550 baskets are the focus of the collection. The baskets come from all over the western United States. The baskets were collected and donated by Marion R. Plummer and Mr. and Mrs. Stanley Plummer, and echo the Heards' basketry collection. The collection was principally developed from the mid 1920s to the 1960s, and contains excellent examples of miniature baskets.

The Museum's southwestern collections were augmented by a 1982 gift from a Tucson resident, Nora Kreps Loerpabel. Ms. Loerpabel donated 200 pieces of Mohave beadwork and ceramics. Many of the ceramics were by the noted Mohave potter, Annie Fields. The collection was well documented as to date of manufacture or collection.

Also in 1982, the Museum received more than 80 examples of Hopi and Navajo weaving from William E. McGee, who was for many years a trader at Keams Canyon, Arizona. These recent examples of Hopi and Navajo woven clothing were primarily from the 1950s and 1960s.

In 1983, the Graham Foundation for Advanced Studies in Fine Arts, located in Chicago, Illinois, donated nearly 200 examples of historic Navajo jewelry. The numerous strands of turquoise and shell arranged in necklaces and earrings are a special feature of the collection.

The Galbraith Collection of American Indian Art is in the process of being donated to the Museum by Henry Galbraith. Mr. Galbraith, a longtime Phoenix businessman and former Trustee of the Museum, amassed the collection with his late wife, Thelma. Mr. Galbraith's donation of more than 420 pieces from an original collection of 1,500 will be an important addition to the Museum's holdings. More than 100 paintings are included, many by early 20th century southwestern American Indian artists whose work is important in the Museum's fine art collection. Hopi silver jewelry is also an important facet of the Galbraith Collection. And, more than one quarter of the gift consists of baskets from the Southwest, California, and the Northwest, with concentrations of Chemehuevi and Pima baskets. The collection also includes Navajo pictorial textiles that are excellent examples of the weaving being done in the 1960s and 1970s. Mr. Galbraith has also donated a comprehensive set of Zuni kachina drawings by Zuni artist Duane Dishta to the Museum's fine art collection.

b.

a.

a. The Plummer Collection contains fine baskets from California, such as the Pomo basket on the left. It is decorated with shell disk beads and quail plumes. The basket on the right is by the Panamint of Death Valley.

b. This traditional Navajo dress, donated by William McGee, consists of identical front and back panels. It was woven in 1960 by Emma Lee who received an award for the quality of her work. The concha belt shown with it was acquired by the Fred Harvey Company in 1937.

The fine art collection of the Museum consists of work done by American Indian artists. The American Indian fine art movement was in an embryonic stage during the early 1900s when Mr. and Mrs. Heard were actively collecting. Only three pieces out of a total of 2,500 in the Museum's collection are recorded as being acquired by the Heards in 1925 and 1926. Those three pieces by the late Hopi artist, Fred Kabotie, are among the finest in the collection.

The collection of art by American Indian artists that is a focal point of the Museum's programs and collecting today began to develop in 1964. In a relatively short time the Museum has assembled a collection with strength in traditional painting from the Southwest and Oklahoma artists, a concentration of

work by Hopi artists, and a growing collection of contemporary art, much of which has appeared in the Museum's Biennial Native American Fine Art Invitational exhibits.

For several years in the 1970s, the Museum also sponsored a juried sculpture competition. American Indian sculpture is a component of the fine art collection that has expanded in very recent years. The Dr. Dean Nichols Sculpture Court and the Shaffer Green offer opportunities to present some of the sculptural works in the Museum collection.

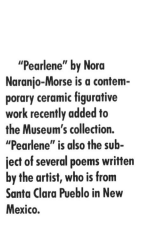

"Pearlene" by Nora Naranjo-Morse is a contemporary ceramic figurative work recently added to the Museum's collection. "Pearlene" is also the subject of several poems written by the artist, who is from Santa Clara Pueblo in New Mexico.

This watercolor painting of eagle dancers by Hopi artist Fred Kabotie was collected by Mrs. Heard in 1925.

Special American Indian Art Collections

The first major gift of American Indian art came to the Museum in 1970 from Dr. and Mrs. Oscar Thoeny. Dr. Thoeny, a Phoenix physician and Trustee of The Heard Museum, contributed 59 paintings to the Museum's fine art collection. The paintings by Southwest and Oklahoma artists are classic works primarily from the 1950s and 1960s.

Kachina drawings were the focus of another collection that is now part of the Museum's fine art holdings. A set of more than 400 drawings by Hopi artist Cliff Bahnimptewa was commissioned by Dr. and Mrs. Dean Nichols. The collection was first exhibited at the Museum in 1971, published, and later donated by Mrs. Nichols, a long-time supporter and Trustee of The Heard Museum. The drawings make an excellent complement to the Museum's collection of kachina dolls. The collection presents images of Hopi Kachinas from the perspective of a resident of Third Mesa on the Hopi Reservation.

The Strickland Collection consists of 300 pieces of American Indian fine art covering a wide range of periods and styles, including excellent examples of works by Oklahoma artists and major works by contemporary artists. The collection was assembled by Dr. Rennard Strickland who is originally from Oklahoma. Dr. Strickland is a noted scholar in the fields of American Indian law and art. The collection is being given to the Museum in annual gifts of which several major donations have been made.

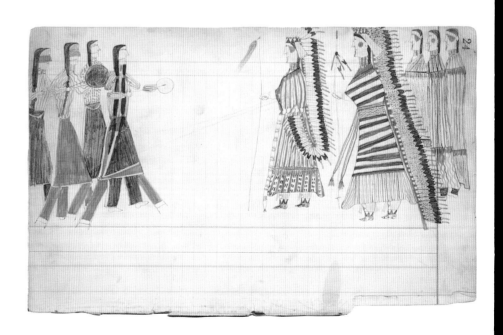

"Women Honoring Warriors," 1875-1880, is by No Horse (Cheyenne-Arapaho). An entire ledger book containing drawings by No Horse was part of a collection of historic artifacts and photographs from the Oklahoma Territory bequeathed to the Museum by the Estate of Carolann Smurthwaite.

"Tall Visitor at Tocito," 1981, by Grey Cohoe (Navajo) comes to the Museum as a part of the Rennard Strickland Collection. (opposite page)

An 1895 manuscript in the Museum archives written by Dwight Heard describes a visit he and Maie made to Chihuahua City in northern Mexico where they purchased a serape. The Heards' attraction to Hispanic design and architecture continued through the early history of the Museum with its largest expression in the Spanish Colonial Revival style of architecture selected for the Museum building and its furnishings.

The Fred Harvey Collection added some important examples of historic Hispanic material to the collection, not the least of which are the Saltillo serapes from Mexico and weavings from 19th century northern New Mexico.

In the years since 1950, the Museum collections have grown to include major acquisitions from American Indian groups in northwestern Mexico and contemporary Mexican ceramics and textiles. This includes contemporary Mexican ceramics assembled in 1979 by the Museo National de Artes in Mexico City. More than 435 ceramics present the major ceramic traditions of Mexican folk art. These acquisitions were made possible by funding from the Phoenix organization, Friends of Mexican Art (FOMA).

In 1971, the Museum purchased more than 325 pieces of clothing from many villages of Guatemala. The clothing, mainly complete costumes, is from the 1960s, and with its documentation is of great importance for the collection.

The Museum has also acquired the Percy Ellis Coe Memorial Collection, which consists of approximately 150 artifacts from cultures of Amazonian Ecuador. Given in 1980 by Mary and Kathryn Coe, the material was collected in 1978-1979 by Mr. Coe's daughter, Kathryn. It contains many examples of ethnographic material including ceramics, barkcloth, tools, and baskets.

This headdress was made by the Achuara Javaroan Indians from Rio Pastaza, Ecuador, of toucan tail feathers. It is from the Coe Collection.

The contemporary ceramic jar is part of a water cooler set from San Blas Atempa, Tehuantepec, Oaxaca. The ceramic candlestick holder has a Noah's Ark motif and is by Adrian Luis Gonzales from Metepec, Mexico. These ceramics were acquired through the support of the Friends of Mexican Art (FOMA). (opposite page)

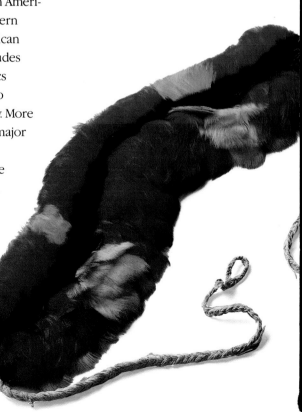

African and Pacific Island Collections

The Museum presents exhibits of art from many parts of the world. Within the collection, African and Pacific art are two focal areas.

Sudanese baskets, a few Egyptian Dynastic artifacts, and North African leather work were part of the Museum's early collection and had decorated the walls of Casa Blanca. The Heards collected on a trip down the Nile in 1926.

Subsequent development of the collection has focused on African art that is generally sub-Saharan, especially from western Africa. Carved figures and masks are the most numerous items in the collection.

More than 100 works from Africa and the Pacific have been added to the Museum's collection through focused donations from Edward Jacobson, Phoenix attorney and Life Trustee of the Museum. Mr. Jacobson has also donated important examples of southwestern craft arts and fine art to the collection. Since 1975, Mr. Jacobson's giving has centered on West African and Melanesian tribal art.

a.

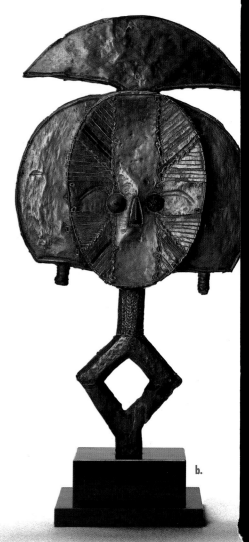

b.

a. These Hawaiian wooden bowls are a few of the Polynesian pieces collected by the Heards. The piece on the left is from the collection of Queen Li-liuokalani, c. 1890.

b. This Kota reliquary figure from Gabon, West Africa, was donated by Life Trustee Edward Jacobson. The Kota use such figures as guardians of ancestral relics.

When visitors came to The Heard Museum in 1929, the library was the first room they encountered as they entered the gate. This primary location of the library underlines the central importance this resource has always had for The Heard Museum. Early records of acquisitions reported to the Board included purchases of books, as well as purchases of artifacts.

In 1987, Dr. Robert I. Schattner donated more than 30,000 volumes that had previously been a portion of the Prescott College Library Special Collections and the personal library of Donald C. Scott, former director of the Peabody Museum, Harvard University.

Today the library is available to the public for research, but holdings are non-circulating. The collection includes books on subjects compatible with the overall Museum focus— southwestern American Indian culture and art, American Indian artists, general American Indian cultural information, tribal art, and anthropology.

The most recent focus of the collection is archival and visual materials. In the coming years, the Museum will augment the book collection with photographic and electronic information relative to a multi-cultural world.

a.

b.

a. The books on Spanish architecture used by the Heards to plan the Museum are part of the library collection. They are marked with the Museum's historic bookplate.

b. Mrs. Heard designed furniture for the Museum, favoring the heavy, dark Spanish Colonial style. Several of the pieces were so well-built that they are in use today in The Heard Museum Library.

This publication is dedicated to Mary M. Brennan, who, as a Museum Trustee and Guild member for 16 years, was The Heard Museum's *communicator* personified. Whether in her volunteer role as an officer of the Board of Trustees, a *bridgebuilder* between the Guild and Museum Board, a Museum guide, or Bookstore *marketeer*, Mary's energy was focused on developing other people's interest in our Museum and Native American cultures. Mary's friendliness, thoughtfulness, and warmth made other volunteers, staff, and Museum visitors feel we were each her special friend.

No one has ever matched Mary's storytelling ability on the same subjects which this booklet is highlighting: our founders; our collections; and our extraordinary volunteers! Mary Brennan was one such Heard Museum volunteer extraordinaire, and with this publication we recognize her generosity and love for The Heard Museum.

Michael J. Fox, Director